paint

---

make

---

create

Learn how to mix painting with other crafts
to create 20 fun seasonal projects

D1372092

paint

make

create

Learn how to mix painting with other crafts
to create 20 fun seasonal projects

BECKI CLARK

*Photographs by Jesse Wild
and Becki Clark*

WHITE OWL

*This book is dedicated to my lovely Mama
who keeps encouraging and inspiring me
with her creativity and kindness.*

First published in Great Britain in 2020 by
PEN & SWORD WHITE OWL
An imprint of Pen & Sword Books Ltd
Yorkshire – Philadelphia

Copyright © Becki Clark, 2020
www.beckiclark.com @becki_clark_

ISBN 9781526793010

The right of Becki Clark to be identified as Author of this work has been asserted by
her in accordance with the Copyright, Designs and Patents Act 1988.

A CIP catalogue record for this book is available from the British Library.

All rights reserved. No part of this book may be reproduced or transmitted in any form
or by any means, electronic or mechanical including photocopying, recording or by any
information storage and retrieval system, without permission from the Publisher in writing.

Group Publisher: Jonathan Wright
Series Editor and Publishing Consultant: Katherine Raderecht
Art Director: Jane Toft
Editor: Katherine Raderecht
Photography: Becki Clark and Jesse Wild

Printed and bound in India by Replika Press Pvt. Ltd.

Pen & Sword Books Ltd incorporates the Imprints of Pen & Sword Books
Pen & Sword Books Limited incorporates the imprints of Atlas, Archaeology, Aviation,
Discovery, Family History, Fiction, History, Maritime, Military, Military Classics, Politics,
Select, Transport, True Crime, Air World, Frontline Publishing, Leo Cooper, Remember
When, Seaforth Publishing, The Praetorian Press, Wharncliffe Local History, Wharncliffe
Transport, Wharncliffe True Crime and White Owl.

For a complete list of Pen & Sword titles please contact:
PEN & SWORD BOOKS LIMITED
47 Church Street, Barnsley, South Yorkshire S70 2AS, England
E-mail: enquiries@pen-and-sword.co.uk
Website: www.pen-and-sword.co.uk
or
PEN AND SWORD BOOKS
1950 Lawrence Rd, Havertown, PA 19083, USA
E-mail: Uspen-and-sword@casematepublishers.com
Website: www.penandswordbooks.com

contents

INTRODUCTION 07

CHAPTER ONE
Materials 09

CHAPTER TWO
Material exercises.................... 13

CHAPTER THREE
Colour 16

CHAPTER FOUR: SPRING
Spring cake topper.................... 22
Abstract collage 28
Ceramic floral eggs 34
Floral embroidery hoop 38
Ditsy plant pots..................... 42

CHAPTER FIVE: SUMMER
Beach bag............................. 48
Aluminium water bottle 52
Wild hedgerow place names 56
Shell jewellery dish 62
Citrus linen tablecloth 66

CHAPTER SIX: AUTUMN
Wabi-sabi candlesticks 72
Graphic clay mobile 76
Leaf printed napkins 80
White painted pumpkins................... 84
Abstract flower vase 88

CHAPTER NINE: WINTER
Modern baubles 94
Classic baubles...................... 98
Foliage crackers 102
Seasonal wall hanging................... 106
Winter wrapping paper 110

RESOURCES
Templates................... 114
FAQ 118
Stockist and resources 119
About the author 120

introduction

Everyone can paint. You might feel you can't, but it really is as simple as picking up a paint brush, dipping it in a palette of paints and making some brush strokes on a page. For a long time I thought I couldn't paint, but I now realise I just had a very particular expectation about what painting should look like.

Then something changed for me; I read about 'the gap' - the imaginary space between where you are as a creative and where you want to be. I was painting but I didn't like what I was making. I had an idea of what I wanted to make but something wasn't quite right. I was never happy because there was a gap between where I was and my taste and expectations for my painting projects. I realised there was no magic wand to close the gap and the only way to close it was to carry on working towards my goal by practicing, perfecting my skill and slowly but surely one day I would make something that felt like me. The gap might open again because you want to expand on your style or creativity, but the only way to bridge the gap is to get started and just get on and do it.

Throughout this book, I hope to inspire you to explore all the wonderful ways to enjoy painting, making and creating seasonally inspired projects without worrying about doing things right or wrong. This book is all about finding joy in mixing colours, finding a palette that makes you happy (which is one of my favourite things to do), working with a range of different paints and learning how to apply them to different surfaces from ceramics to fabric.

My work is mostly inspired by the seasons so the projects reflect the excitement, colour and feeling of the natural world which is a constant and abundant source of inspiration for me, my paintings, work and craft projects.

HOW TO USE THIS BOOK

In the next few chapters we'll explore the materials you need to get started, basic colour theory, colour palettes and a few simple exercises to help you feel confident with your paint brush and paint. You'll find some simple motifs and patterns to paint to help you work through the twenty seasonally inspired projects in the second half of the book. Each project focuses on combining painting with other crafts in a celebration of the seasons.

You also don't need to complete the chapters chronologically. Just work through the exercises and projects that grab your attention first. Start with what excites you most and use that excitement to push yourself out of your comfort zone and pick up the paint brush.

chapter one: materials

Let's start with some of the materials I will be using throughout the book. For beginner painters, it is not essential to buy all the different types of paint mentioned here, however for some projects specific paint types are required.

With great adhesive qualities and versatility, acrylics are great for craft and mixed media projects

Watercolours have a much looser feel to them than acrylics. How much you dilute them affects their colour and transparency

PAINTS

Acrylic Paint

Acrylic paints are an essential item in your painting kit; they are one of the most versatile paints when it comes to craft projects because they will adhere to most surfaces including paper, wood, fabric and ceramic. When using acrylic paint you can create different effects by adding more water to make the colours more opaque. Acrylic paint dries quickly which means it is useful for creating layers of colours.

Watercolour Paint

Watercolour is the most delicate paint, known for it's subtlety. Traditionally used on paper, watercolours can be used to create washes and transparent colours. Watercolour is a popular medium for painting botanical subjects because of the delicate and free flowing style you can create with it. Watercolours are available in pans and tubes. I personally like to use pans as I find them easier to work with and less wasteful.

Fabric Paint

Fabric paints are specially designed for painting directly onto fabrics. Some brands of fabric paint need to be heat set to make your design washable. The consistency of fabric paint is similar to acrylic paint and you'll find a huge variety, from heavier opaque paint right through to the glow in the dark.

PAINT MARKERS

Using Posca Markers is one of the less traditional methods of painting but they are one of my favourite materials to use. The Posca Markers we will use throughout this book are water proof and water resistant and suitable for a range of surfaces from

My go-to are the 5mm point Posca Paint Markers, perfect for getting full coverage on projects

The 3 brushes we will be using throughout the book are great for beginners and come in a wide variety of different sizes

glass, ceramic, paper and fabric. They are flexible and easy to use.

It is not essential to have all the different paints. If you have an odd tube of acrylic paint, a pan of watercolours or a few Posca Marker Pens in your craft stash, just experiment using what you have. For many projects this will be fine. However, some projects will require specialist paints depending on the surface you are painting on.

PAINT BRUSHES

There are a huge variety of paint brushes available, however for the exercises in this book you don't need to rush out and buy every single one. In fact, if you have some paint brushes lying around, just use them. If you need to buy some brushes, here's a guide to what to invest in.

Round brushes – these have a pointed tip and the bristles are close together so you can work on detailed paintings.

Flat brushes – these work well for covering larger surfaces with colour; they spread paint quickly and evenly and are great for washes and mark making.

Filbert brush – these are flat brushes with a rounded top. These brushes work well for coverage and also help create a more detailed look than flat brushes because they are easier to manipulate around corners.

If you are completely new to painting, I have included a list of materials at the back of the book to help you choose what to buy for your new painter's kit.

chapter two: material exercises

In this chapter you will a few simple introductory exercises to get you started using the different types of paints we will be using throughout the book. If you are new to painting, start on paper before you move on to other surfaces. This will allow you to best see the consistency, style and way you work with the paints.

Materials

■ Posca Paint Marker 5mm

■ Card

EXPLORING POSCA PAINT MARKERS

The reason I have included paint markers in this book is because I use them for a lot of craft projects. You can create precise bold shapes and the rounded nib of the pen automatically helps you create smoother lines than those you make using a bristle brush. They are also great for working on a variety of surfaces that other paints are less easy to apply onto.

Creating shapes

The first exercise is to create some simple shapes with your marker pen. Take a look at the image above and try and draw similar abstract shapes. Although it feels more like drawing than painting, the effect you will create is like that of an acrylic or gouache paint.

Overlapping colour

The next exercise is to work one colour over another. Start with a lighter colour and draw three leaf shapes pointing upwards and colour them in. Once they are dry, you can add the circle berry shapes in a darker colour layering over the lighter blue leaves.

Creating pattern

Now lets try creating a pattern with just a few simple shapes. Draw the foliage shape above around your page looking at how the shapes work together to form a pattern. Create a few sheets of these with the foliage close together or further apart for different effects.

Materials

- Daler-Rowney Graduate acrylic paint
- Daler-Rowney flat brush
- Pot of water
- Multimedia paper or card

EXPLORING ACRYLIC PAINT

These exercises are aimed at exploring acrylic colours and focus on colour blocking and layering paint. I find acrylic the easiest paint to work with when painting bold shapes, defined lines and painting colour over colour, especially when working on more unusual surfaces.

You will learn how acrylic paint reacts with water, work one colour over the top of another and find out how to create the right consistency of paint to achieve a splatter effect. When you are working with layers of acrylic paint, you will need to let each layer dry before changing colour to avoid mixing the colours together. Gouache paint has very similar properties to acrylic paint if you already own a set.

Exploring consistency

The first exercise is to create a few swatches of colour to get used to how acrylic paint interacts with water. Start by using a dry brush to create a swatch of colour with the paint. Then slowly add increasing amounts of water and make more swatches to get used to the different opacities you can create by watering the paint down.

Building colour

In the next exercise, you will learn to work colours over each other to create clearly defined blocks. First paint a rectangle on the page in a light colour. Then, using a darker colour, paint a circle over the rectangle. Let each layer dry before applying the next colour. Finally, paint a semi circle over both shapes to create the pattern.

Creating an effect

The final technique to learn is paint splattering. Try different ways to create splatters by dipping your brush in paint and then shaking it over your paper. If you have lots of room you can vigorously flick the paint across the paper, but in a smaller space just hold the brush over the paper and tap the brush near the end to create splatters.

Materials:

- Winsor & Newton watercolour paint pan

- Daler-Rowney flat brush

- Pot of water

- Watercolour paper

EXPLORING WATERCOLOUR PAINT

The best way to start your journey with watercolour paints is to learn how to create washes of paint. Creating washes is a fun exercise to do. There is no right way your wash should look; it depends on the amount of paint pigment on the paper.

Choose colours to work with that are bright and bold so you can see how the pigment changes as you dilute it with increasing amounts of water as you work through these exercises. If you want to mix colours, I would advise investing in a small enamel bowl or mixing tray, rather than mixing colours in your watercolour pans.

Paint washes

To create a strong bold colour wash, dip a flat brush into a pot of water, removing any excess by tapping it gently. You want the brush to hold enough water for the colour to be evenly pigmented when you dip it into the paint. Drag the brush across the paper. Go back over the same stroke to create a more intense wash.

Water based washes

To create this effect, use a clean brush to spread water over your paper. Dip the brush into the paint pan and transfer the paint into the middle of the pool of water on your paper. Let the paint slowly spread into the water. You can help the paint along or just see what effect you create by letting the pigment mix with the water.

Ombré effects

To create an ombré effect (the blending of one colour hue to another, from dark to light), pick up water on your brush, tap off any excess and paint a bold line at the top of the page. Add more water and paint to your brush and drag it downwards. Finally, add more water to create the lightest shade in the ombré pattern.

chapter three: colour

Colour will play a big part in your painting and crafting journey. The colour palettes you choose can completely change the mood and feel of a piece. A basic understanding of colour theory is a great place to start, but remember to just focus on the joy and feeling of the colours - that is what you want in your work!

THE COLOUR WHEEL

Colour theory is an incredibly complex subject and a book in itself! To get started with the painting exercises and projects in this book, you just need a basic understanding of the colour wheel. You'll probably be familiar the concept of the colour wheel, which was developed in the 17th century to show how colours relate to each other. The colour wheel visually demonstrates the relationship between primary, secondary and tertiary colours and has been instrumental in helping artists to explain colour relationships and to develop colour schemes. The three primary colours are red, blue and yellow. Combining any two of those colours will give you one of the secondary colours: Red and blue make violet, yellow and blue make green, and red and yellow make orange. A third set of colours, the tertiary colours, fill in the six gaps between the primary and secondary colours: red-orange, blue-green, red-violet and so on. Using the red, blue and yellow primary colours you can mix any of the other colours on the wheel. Using a colour wheel is a good way for you to understand the result of mixing one colour paint with another colour.

Black and white are known as neutral colours and are used in this book to add to other colours to darken or lighten them or to act as accent colours on pieces.

HUES

Hue very basically means colour. A hue refers to the dominant colour family of the specific colour you're looking at. So, for example, the hue of navy would be blue and the hue of mustard would be yellow. Think of the hue as one of the six primary and secondary colours; the underlying base colour of the mixture you're looking at is either yellow, orange, red, violet, blue or green.

COMPLEMENTARY COLOURS

Complementary colours are two colours that are on the opposite sides of the colour wheel. The high contrast of complementary colours creates a vibrant look especially when used at full saturation. Complementary colours can be difficult to use in large doses, but work well when you want something to stand out and create impact.

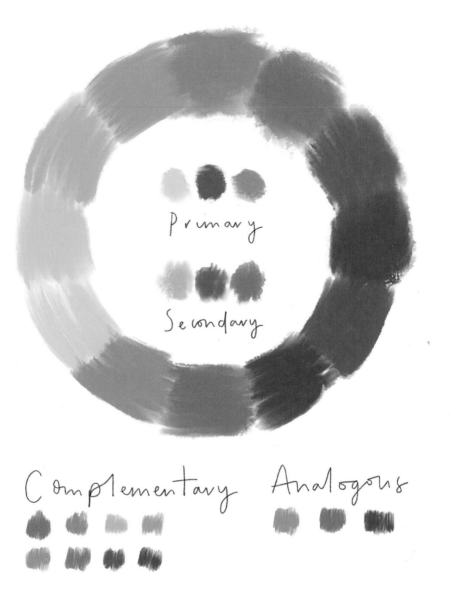

Primary

Secondary

Complementary   Analogous

ANALOGOUS COLOURS

Analogous colours are groups of three colours that are next to each other on the colour wheel, and a tertiary. Red, orange, and red-orange are examples. They usually match well and create a serene and comfortable effect. Analogous colour schemes are often found in nature and are harmonious and pleasing to the eye.

When I choose a colour palette I tend to use complementary or analogous colours to find something that works for the piece. You will probably find that you do this naturally without realising. I think it's useful to understand the theory of colours but, when painting, it's all about using colours that make you feel joyful and happy.

I tend to have phases of using particular colours. If I discover a new palette, I find I will become absolutely obsessed with those colours and spend weeks painting with them before moving on. I have also come to realise that the seasons really impact my choice of colours. For me it's more about the feeling a particular season gives me, rather than the traditional colours associated with that season; for example, terracotta and olive green for autumn.

In the last few years, in March, I have become obsessed with pink and green, inspired by the arrival of spring and the feeling of new beginnings and hope it gives me. To connect to your painting you have to find a colour palette that makes you feel joyful and creates positive creative emotions.

To experiment with making colour palettes, start by creating a colour chart from your paint set. Pictured are watercolours from Winsor & Newton, but this technique works for all paints. Swatch each of the colours in your sketchbook and number each colour. Explore mixing these colours together to create new colours. Keep a note of which colours you mixed by using the number system so when you want to make the colour again you know how. This is about learning how different colours mix together and which colours you want to create your projects.

Creating inspiring palettes

First find an image or object you like. This can come from anywhere - nature, flowers, fashion, interiors - just find a picture that inspires you. Take a minute to examine your image to determine what the main colours are. In the image opposite, you can see that the dominant colours are green, white and pink. Now note the tone of the colours - these are all the same soft chalky muted colour and it's that which makes them work together so well. Have a go at finding a few images or objects and creating colour palettes with your paints from them. It will take trial and error to get it right and you may need to experiment with more mixing to create the exact colours from your image but this is the most important exercise in the book to get right, so persevere.

Re-imagining colours

We have so many preconceived ideas about what colours certain things 'should' be. As an illustrator, I think its important to think outside the box to test your creativity. For example, our preconceived notion is that a Christmas wreath has green leaves. However, put that aside and have fun experimenting with other colours and you will fire your imagination and start a more interesting creative journey. Try this exercise and have some fun.

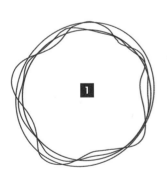

1. Start by drawing round a cup on a piece of A5 card to make a circle. Take your first colour and paint three lines entwining around your circular shape

2. Add small leaves in the same colour around the three lines
3. Using a second colour of your choice, add more leaves into the gaps in your wreath

4. Add in small berry shapes (dots) in clusters of three around the leaves in a third colour
Try different colour ways to see how the design changes

These exercises will help you find colours and palettes that make you happy. Painting should bring you joy so by finding a joyful colour palette before you begin it is a great place to start.

chapter four: spring

For me, the longing for spring usually starts in February. After the excitement of the festive season and a period of reflection in January, I am ready for the arrival of the first flowers and green leaves on the trees. Spring brings new inspiration and a chance to celebrate warmer days. I love to eat cake in the garden, plant seedlings, take my camera out on long walks in the countryside and create unique pieces of artwork for my home. Here you will learn to create collages, decorate ceramics and enjoy combining painting with textiles to celebrate the joy and colour of spring.

cake topper

Create and paint your own meadow-inspired cake toppers, perfect for birthday cakes, Mother's Day or just a springtime celebration. The great thing about these cute paper cake toppers is that you'll be able to keep reusing them for celebrations with friends and family in the years to come.

Materials:

- 200gsm coloured cards
- 300gsm card for backing
- Acrylic paint - I used black, yellow and white
- Pencil
- Scissors
- Super Glue
- Paint brush
- Kebab sticks for large cake topper
- Cocktail sticks for the mini toppers

BECKI'S TIPS

- Use a mix of colours so your shapes stand out. The florals work well with the different greens because the colours really pop out!

- Measure your cake before making your topper. Just pop the kebab sticks in the cake and measure the distance between them to get the length of the topper

23

1. Decide on your colour palette. As this is a spring cake topper, I've chosen colours inspired by wild flower meadows, filled with cornflowers and daisies with lots of fresh greens to celebrate the season. Choose your colours based on the season you are making your toppers for to get the right feeling.

2. Start by cutting out templates from page 116. Use a mix of sizes of the different floral shapes to help create a more whimsical wild feel. Think about making clusters of smaller flowers to surround the bigger shapes. Here, I used three of the largest flowers and a mix of 11 of the medium and small.

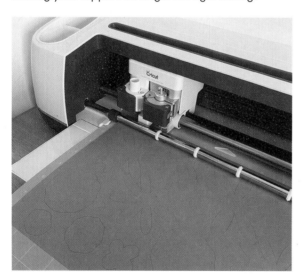

3. If you own a Cricut or other die-cutting machine you can use this to cut out your shapes. However, as they are such simple shapes, cutting them out with scissors or a craft knife will work just as well.

4. Once you have cut out all your paper flower heads, add your painted detail. Using a small round brush and black acrylic paint, create a circle into the centre of each flower shape. Then add smaller dots around the centre using the tip of the brush.

5. You might also want to paint more modern and graphic looking centres by painting circles with concentric lines radiating out from them. Paint a mix of black and white centres on the coloured card to create interesting contrast.

6. If you want to add more depth to your flowers use light colours to paint details onto the petals. You might want to add a little more water to the white for a subtle look. If you use the round brush you will add texture to each of the strokes.

7. Create the backing card structure for the flowers by cutting a piece of card to the desired width of your topper. Fold the ends over the kebab sticks and glue in place with the Super Glue.

8. When the glue is dry, cut the topper using small craft scissors to give it a more arched shape. This will help create the gentle undulating look of a country meadow for your coloured flowers.

9. Cut out leaves from the templates on page 116 in different coloured green card. Play around with the placement of the leaves before sticking them in place. Keep the leaves around the edges of your card and leave enough space in the middle for your flowers.

10. Now you can start sticking your floral shapes down. Cluster them together and create a 3D effect by bending any larger petals upwards. If you crease the card you will find they stay in shape without you having to secure them with glue.

11. Keep the topper looking balanced by using one of the larger flowers as a centre focal point and clustering the flowers around it. Work out your arrangement before you glue them in place.

12. Continue to add smaller flowers around the focal point until you are happy with your topper layout. Layer your flowers and leaves to create an impactful paper meadow! You're ready to add to your cake.

If you have some flowers left over or you want to decorate cup cakes instead, simply use single cocktail sticks for each flower or create mini clusters of flowers and leaves on each stick

A FLOWER BOOK
FOR THE POCKET
SKENE

HOORAY!

WEDDING FLOWERS

abstract collage

One of the things I love most about spring is cleaning and refreshing my house after the winter months. Moving things around or popping a new print up on the wall is lovely way to refresh the space for the new season. Creating your own collage artwork is the perfect way to make your home unique.

Materials:

- 300gsm white card
- 170gsm paper
- Scissors
- Glue
- Acrylic paint
- Flat paint brush
- Mixing tray
- Pot of water

BECKI'S TIPS

- What your print looks like will depend on your own taste and style. If you find it easier, use my design as guide to get you started. Take your time choosing your colour pallet. Collaging is a really mindful activity; just let your creativity flow

- Start with bigger pieces of painted paper to make the project seem less daunting

- Use coloured card for your background for extra colour

- Stick with washi tape directly on to your walls

1. Begin by choosing your colour palette. I chose pink and green tones to symbolise the arrival of spring. Ideally choose a maximum of three colours to give your collage a cohesive look. You can use different tones of each hue to keep it cohesive.

2. Experiment by making colour blocks on your 170gsm paper until you find your preferred colours. Create blocks of painted colour on the paper. Don't worry about being neat or creating the same sized blocks because you are going to cut the colours out.

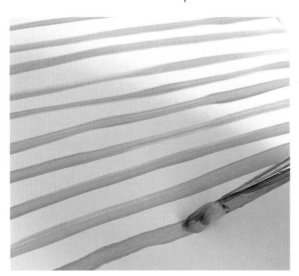

3. Next you need to create some colourful stripes across your page. By adding pressure to your paint brush as you work across the paper, you will create a range of thick and thin lines. You can also create interesting textures by letting the brush run out of paint as it glides across the page.

4. Gingham patterns are fun and easy to create. In the same way as the stripes, you can create thick and thin patterns and explore how the brush creates textures. There are no rules for making creative collages; it is all about using your materials to create something unique.

5. Keep creating different marks and shapes and explore painting dense and sparse patterns with the paint. Different sized spots and dashes work well for simple repeat patterns.

6. Once you are happy with your mark making sheets, leave them to dry thoroughly. Make sure the colours work well together and you have a good selection of different sized shapes to make your collage with.

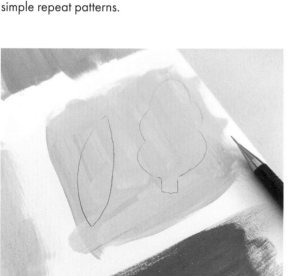

7. Now it's time to cut out your shapes. You can use the templates on page 115 to draw around your sheets of marks. Simple shapes work well - circles which can then be cut in half, squares, rectangles and scalloped lines are particularly good.

8. Now it's time to assemble your artwork. Take a sheet of 300gsm card and get your shapes and glue ready. Start to explore which shapes and colours might work well together for your collage.

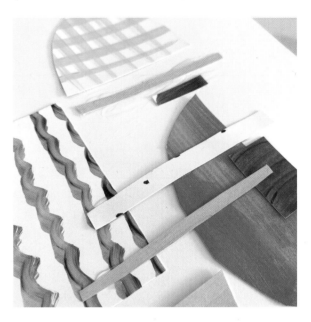

9. Begin placing your shapes onto the card,. Groups of three shapes work well visually so start with 3 of the bigger shapes as a base. Don't glue them down until you are happy with the composition.

10. Layer the smaller patterned shapes over the top of the bigger ones. Start to glue the shapes in place as the more layers you build on top of each other, the harder it is to take your collage apart without ruining the design.

11. If you have lots of shapes, you can create a number of collages at the same time. This is also a really good way to explore the shapes and patterns.

with more freedom. Once all your pieces are glued in place, let the artwork dry before framing and putting up on your wall.

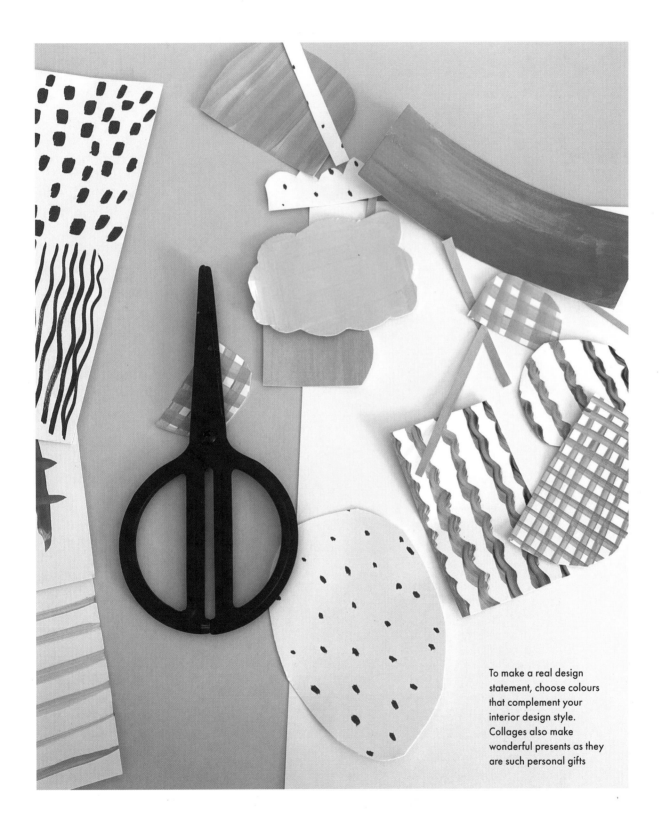

To make a real design statement, choose colours that complement your interior design style. Collages also make wonderful presents as they are such personal gifts

ceramic floral eggs

Paint your own floral eggs to hang in your home, decorate your shelves or gift to a friend as springtime treat. By combining a few simple shapes you can create ditsy floral patterns as well as larger motifs to decorate your eggs. Hang them with a pretty ribbon for a perfect Easter decoration!

Materials:

■ Ceramic Easter eggs

■ Gouache or acrylic paint for a more opaque finish or watercolour paints for a softer look in pink, white, blue, green and yellow

■ Small round paint brush (I used the Daler-Rowney Gold Taklon Brush size1)

■ Pot of water

■ Mixing tray

■ Pencil

BECKI'S TIPS

■ Let each layer of your painting dry. If you work over colours too quickly they'll blend together

■ Spray paint your eggs first if you want a bright base colour

■ Pop your eggs into an eggcup to make it easier to paint them

■ Gouache or acrylic paint will cover pencil lines. Use lighter pencil lines with watercolours

1. Choose your colour palette and, if you are using tube paints, put your paints in a tray. Use a pencil to draw your first motif shapes around the egg. The motifs for this first design are made up of simple curved lines and 'flower heads' made from three-point shapes.

2. Apply your first layer of paint, using a mid-blue for the heads of the flowers and a darker blue for the stem and leaves. Be careful not to smudge the paint as you turn the egg around to paint all the surfaces.

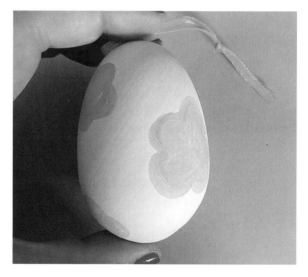

3. Once the initial layer is dry you can use a lighter colour to add the detail into the motif. Use the small round brush to paint three lines from the stalk up to the flower head and through the centre of each leaf.

4. The second design has larger motifs, painted in light pink and varying in size around the egg. Think of this motif as the kind of flower style you are taught to draw in primary school with big scalloped petals.

5. With a mid to dark blue, paint small dots in the centre of your flower shapes, ideally keeping the dot quite small to give a modern ditsy feel to the pattern. Add leave shapes between each flower shape. The leaves don't need to be attached to the flowers.

6. The last design is made up of one single motif which takes up one whole side of the ceramic egg. Start by painting a vertical line from the top to the bottom of the egg, and then add two lines either side at roughly a 45 degree angle to create branches.

7. Add small leaf shapes on each of the four branches. Take your time with these, making sure your paint brush is small enough to be able to paint them accurately. It is important that the smallest leaf still has a really nice defined shape.

8. Add your floral shape to the top of the branches with a light shade of pink. The shape is four tear drops joined together at the top of the stem. Add small pink dots along the foliage. Once the flower is dry, use a darker colour to add detail lines at the bottom of the flower head. Your three eggs are done.

floral embroidery hoop

Give your painterly florals a touch of texture by combining painting and embroidery to make this pretty hoop. This is the perfect Sunday afternoon craft; start by painting your fabric and letting it dry in the spring sunshine before cosying up on the sofa with a cup of tea, needle and thread.

Materials:

■ Embroidery hoop

■ Embroidery thread in your chosen colours (I used the DMC skeins)

■ Embroidery needle

■ Fabric paint

■ Flat paint brush

■ Pot of water

■ Linen or other embroidery fabric (try something without too much texture)

■ Cardboard

■ Glue

BECKI'S TIPS

■ Try a small hoop to begin with if you are a beginner

■ Practice painting your motif shapes on paper before working on fabric. You should also practice your stitches on an off cut of fabric before you start

■ Linen works well as the paint is absorbed well in the material to create nice opaque motifs

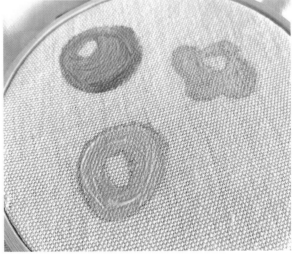

1. Start by securing your fabric in your hoop and choosing your colour palette. For this project, I chose classic pinks and greens, but this design would look great in any colour combination.

2. Using a small paint brush, begin painting your floral motifs in the middle of the hoop. The two shapes on the left are simple circles with holes in the middle and the petal shape on the right is painted using four semi circles joined together.

3. Next paint the leaf shapes. I have used one shade of green, but you can use several different greens if you want a more colourful look. Try a mix of sizes and work your way out from the centre of the design. You don't want anything too close to the edges of the hoop or it will be too hard to stitch onto.

4. Finally, add dots as floral buds around the design. You can paint as many as you like; it really depends on your personal taste. The key thing is to keep the design centred and use a cluster of three painted flowers as your main point of focus. When you are happy with the design, let the paint dry.

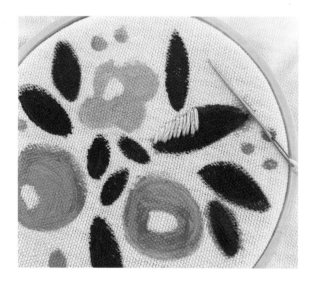

5. Once it is dry, you can begin to embellish your design with embroidery. Use a simple long stitch in contrasting colours to add texture. Long stitch offers a quick way to cover an area of fabric to create an intense colour.

6. Using the painting as your guide, long stitch horizontally across one half of each leaf. Take a contrasting colour and stitch vertically down the leaf to give an interesting texture to your design.

7. Here you can see the combination of vertical and horizontal stitches in two different greens on the leaves create an interesting 3D texture. Embroider half the leaves on the design and leave the rest.

8. Use yellow thread to stitch across the unpainted flower centres. You can add more stitching to the flowers if you prefer, but I like the combination of strong painterly 'petals' and the embroidered centre.

9. Use the light pink thread to work smaller long stitches over a few of the berries. You can also embroider areas that aren't painted. I added a few smaller stitched berries in some of the empty spaces to ensure the design looked balanced.

10. Once you are happy with your design, cut the excess material from around the hoop. You can cut a piece of cardboard the same size as your design and glue to the back to tidy it up and make sure there are no stitches or excess threads on show.

ditsy plant pots

Upcycle any old terracotta pots you have lying around with pretty ditsy floral patterns and give them a new lease of life. These mini planters make the perfect home for cress, seedlings or even spring herbs to display and use in your kitchen. The perfect pots to celebrate spring.

Materials:

- ■ Terracotta pots
- ■ Pencil
- ■ Posca Paint Markers in white, navy and mid blue
- ■ Varnish (optional)

BECKI'S TIPS

- ■ Draw your pattern first on paper if you are anxious about painting straight onto terracotta

- ■ If you don't have Posca Paint Markers, you can use acrylic or gouache paints. They will also create an opaque look on the terracotta

- ■ If you are planning on putting soil into the pots then add a lining. Tin foil cut to the right size is perfect

- ■ Varnish the pots if you want to make sure your design is waterproof

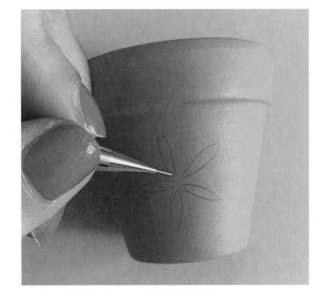

1. The first pattern in this design is based on repeat florals; created with small simple shapes. You will need the white and navy Paint Markers. First draw the five point flower using elongated ovals with a circle left in the middle. Think of how you were taught to draw flowers when you were a child.

2. Using the white Paint Marker fill in the petal shapes around your pot. To get the look of a complete pattern, make sure some of your flowers bleed 'off' the sides of the pot. This means you will have some half flower shapes on the edges of your pot.

3. Taking one of the blue Paint Markers, draw small circles in the centre of the flower shapes to complete your floral motifs. The smaller the circle in the centre of the flower, the 'ditzier' the pattern will look.

4. The second design consists of a motif made up of three circles clustered next to each other in the middle of the pot. Next, sketch leaf shapes working outwards from the cluster of circles.

5. Taking the white Paint Marker, fill in the circles. I have drawn three different sized circles as it's much easier than trying to make them all the same size.

6. Colour in the leaf shapes with the navy blue Paint Marker. Once your white circles have dried you can add a small circle and three smaller dots on them.

7. The third pot is covered in lots of smaller versions of the design you created in steps 5 and 6. Using smaller shapes gives a ditsy floral look to your design.

8. Using navy blue, add leaf shapes working in different directions from your florals. You don't want the flowers to look too structured in a ditsy pattern.

9. The final pattern is inspired by my love of daisies. Use lines working out from the centre to create your petal shapes and repeat over the pot mixing the sizes of the florals.

10. Create the centre of your daisies using the navy Paint Marker. If there are any awkward spaces, just add smaller ones in to act as fillers. Your pots are done!

chapter five: summer

Summer is all about bright bold colours that make your heart sing and warm evenings eating dinner in the garden with friends and family. I like to focus on practical crafts in the summer so in this chapter, there's a painted beach bag, shell inspired jewellery holders and a pretty way to upcycle your water bottle with a jazzy tropical design. You'll also learn to create your own painterly embroidered table linen and make personalised place names, inspired by my love of blue china, to jazz up your alfresco dining table. The techniques used in these summer projects can be used throughout other seasons too using different colour palettes.

beach bag

Everyone has an old tote bag hanging around that could do with a makeover. Using a simple masking technique you can create a geometric painterly bag design perfect for beach evenings or summer picnics. Choose your own colour palette for a unique take on this simple upcycle.

Materials:

- Canvas tote bag
- Masking tape
- Fabric paint in at least 3 colours (I used Tulip Fabric Paint)
- Flat paint brush
- Pot of water

BECKI'S TIPS

- Clean your brush thoroughly between paint colours. The key to this project looking professional is clear definition between your paint colours

- If you are upcycling an old tote bag, wash and dry it before applying the fabric paint

1. Iron your canvas bag so that you have crease free material to work with. This is important so that the paint can be applied easily and evenly. Stick your first piece of masking tape across the whole diagonal length of the bag.

2. Use this diagonal line of tape as a guideline for positioning smaller triangles across the bag. Placement of the tape isn't permanent so you can play around with the positioning until you are happy with your design.

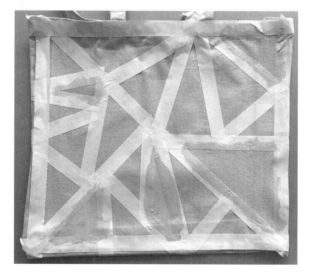

3. Continue to create your design, using existing shapes as guidelines until the whole bag is covered with masking tape triangles. To keep your design neat and easier to paint, tape off the outside edges of the bag so you will only be painting flat fabric.

4. Taking a medium sized flat brush, begin painting the peach colour over a random selection of the triangle shapes. The paint will absorb into the bag so you will need to spread it quickly across the areas, moving your brush smoothly.

5. Once you've applied the peach colour and you are happy with the look, paint in the other sections with pink and blues. It doesn't matter if the painting smudges over the masking tape, but just make sure it doesn't seep into any other colours.

6. When you have finished your design, leave the bag to dry. If you want to speed up the drying process, you can use a hairdryer, holding it about 20cm away from the bag. To ensure the bag is dry, check with your fingers.

7. Now the fun part! Beginning with the last piece of masking tape you applied, peel it away from the bag, repeating until you are left with your perfect painterly design on your bag, all ready to use.

aluminium water bottle

*Aluminium water bottles are getting more popular and most definitely jazzier
with their patterns nowadays. Why not enjoy an afternoon upcycling a plain
bottle into a tropical themed masterpiece? Ideal for popping in your bag to take
to the beach or to work to keep you hydrated in the hot summer months.*

Materials:

- Aluminium water bottle
- Posca Paint Markers in navy, green, yellow, red, black and white
- Varnish

BECKI'S TIPS

- This project requires a bit of confidence! It is harder working on a curved surface and pencil won't show up on the aluminium so you might want to practice the motifs on a piece of paper first

- If you are pressed for time, you can use these motifs to create a simpler pattern. A repeat of the green leaves around the bottle would look great especially with a pink background!

- If you make a mistake you can wipe the bottle down with soapy water and a cloth and you will be ready to start again

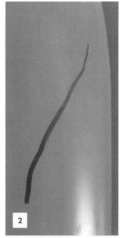

1. Make sure your aluminium bottle is clean and dry ready to work on. You can use any base colour for your bottle design. I just love the tropical vibes of this hot pink and I think it works really well with the leafy design.

2. Decide on your base leaf colour and draw your first line. You can see the line isn't straight or curved but more of a wobbly line. Make it about 10cm long using one continuous stroke with the Paint Marker.

3. This line will act as your stem. Paint the outlines of the leaf shapes on either side of the stem, working outwards and ending with a leaf at the top of the stem.

53

4. Colour in the leaf shapes. The great thing about Paint Marker pens is that they create perfect lines to fill in with colour. Take your time so your lines are as neat and tidy as possible.

5. Repeat this motif across the bottle taking care to make sure it is dry before putting it down. Don't worry too much about the space between the motifs; you can fill these in later with other smaller designs.

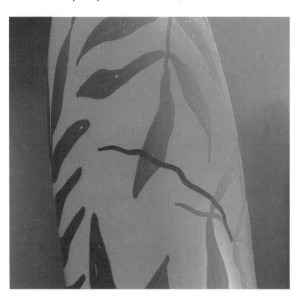

6. Using the navy Paint Marker, draw another line to act as a stem for your next motif. As long as any previous paints are dry, you will be able to paint over them without the paint smudging.

7. Once again, draw leaf shapes along the stem of the leaf with an outline and then colour them in. Repeat this across the surface of the bottle. For reference, I painted five navy sprigs on my bottle.

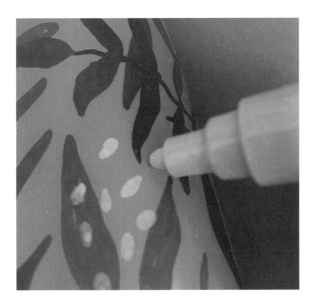

8. Using the yellow Paint Marker, paint large dots in the gaps and over the leaves to create an abstract style and give a pop of colour. Make groups of ten spots about 6 times over the bottle.

9. You can then add large white ovals to give another pop of colour. Group them together in threes and paint randomly across the bottle to give a bit more depth and contrast to the design.

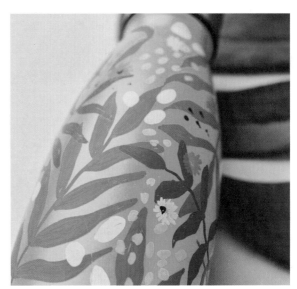

10. Add cactus flowers using a red or lighter pink Paint Marker. Cactus plants are made by painting small spiky circles. These shapes work well for any awkward gaps in your design.

11. Take the black Paint Marker and add dots to the centres of the spiky floral shapes. Once you are happy with your tropical pattern, leave to dry and then spray with varnish to ensure it is waterproof.

wild hedgerow place names

Paint your own wild hedgerow inspired watercolour place names, perfect for summer evenings with friends and family in the garden. I love any excuse to get out the linen tablecloth, pick some garden flowers and create a magical summer evening table setting for no other reason that it brings me joy!

Materials:

- Folded place cards in ivory
- Navy watercolour pan (Winsor & Newton)
- Small fine round brush
- Pencil
- Ruler

BECKI'S TIPS

You don't have to stick to one colour for these place cards. Bear in mind though that watercolours when placed very close together do have a tendency to blend very easily together. Just be wary working on small items like place name cards and make sure each colour is dry before adding the next.

Place a piece of scrap paper underneath the place cards whilst painting so that you can paint off the bottom of the card

Leave the place cards flat when drying to ensure the paint doesn't run

Practice on scrap paper before you start

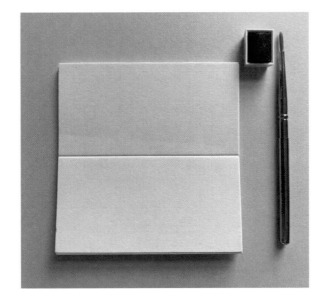

1. Measure the half way point of the card and mark it using a light pencil mark. This allows you to see what area you have to create your design on. Your design will need to sit on the fold point and you need to leave room for the name.

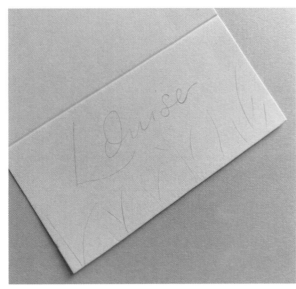

2. Handwrite your chosen name in pencil on the card and then sketch out 3-4cm long curved lines from the bottom. These are your stems. Group pairs of stems together with space in-between them across the whole width of the card.

3. Although you are using watercolour for this project, you don't want the paint consistency to be overly watery. After dipping your brush into the water, tap off the excess before picking up the paint pigment to avoid dripping paint. Paint in the curved lines.

4. The floral effect is made up of lots of small free flowing marks made with the paint brush. Using the tip of the brush, pick up paint from the pan and paint little flick marks coming out of the curved lines you have just made.

5. Experiment with the lengths of the flicks along the curved line. Just using small delicate lines you can begin to build a foliage shape. Remember to keep your flicks all heading in the same direction.

6. You can also use the tip of the paint brush to gently dab small circles along the curved lines to create little berries and buds along the foliage line. Make some bigger than others to create movement in the design.

7. Work across the width of the place name card, alternating between the different marks, to create the feel of a free flowing wild hedgerow.

8. Go back and make little upward strokes at the base of the name place card to create the impression of grass along the bottom edge.

9. Once you are happy with your border, paint over the pencilled name in the same colour. Remember to use a small round brush as the painting and lettering should have a delicate and light feel to it which is easier to achieve with a finer paint brush.

10. If you are feeling confident with the hedgerow design why not try a more floral border for an alternative place card? Start, as before, by painting curved lines from the base of your card to act as the stems of your flowers.

11. To paint flowers, use the tip of the brush and lightly paint swirl shapes (imagine the as e-shapes to begin with). Add the next layer of the flower by painting a curved line around the e-shape.

12. Make another curved line opposite the first one to create the impression of summer roses. As you paint, keep in mind how roses look with their petals all encasing one another.

13. Paint a few roses across your row of stems. Once you get into the swing of painting them it will become easy and natural to do. Have a practice on some spare paper before you work onto your place names.

14. Create leaf shapes along the stems by making two curved lines. As with the previous design, you can add a grass border along the bottom and buds and foliage to fill in the design.

The best thing about these name place cards is that they can all be unique. Mix and match the motifs you like best and each hedgerow border will look like a tiny masterpiece for your guests to take home

shell jewellery dish

Craft your own slice of the ocean to keep your precious stones and pearls safe. Inspired by my love of the seaside these jewellery dish holders are the perfect make to practice your splatter painting technique on. They are also a gorgeous make to gift to friends and family as their very own keepsakes.

Materials:

■ Fimo Professional modelling clay in white

■ Shell cutter (mine was 3.2 x 3.2"/8x8cm)

■ Acrylic paint

■ Flat paint brush

■ Pot of water

■ Rolling pin

■ Spatula

■ Spare paper

BECKI'S TIPS

■ If you want to waterproof your design, use a spray varnish once the paint is dry

■ This technique could be adapted for any shape cutter. Look for cutters in all sorts of shapes from hearts to stars

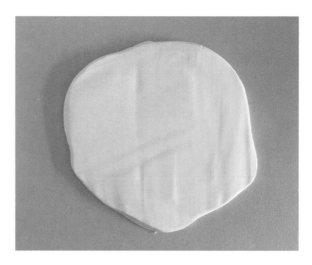

1. Begin with preheating your oven to 100°C/212°F. Take a piece of Fimo about the size of a golf ball and roll it your hands until it is smooth, making sure the surface is clean and dust free.

2. Roll out the Fimo to 1-2cm thickness with a rolling pin. I find it easier to make one dish at a time rather than rolling out a larger piece and cutting into smaller pieces for multiple dishes.

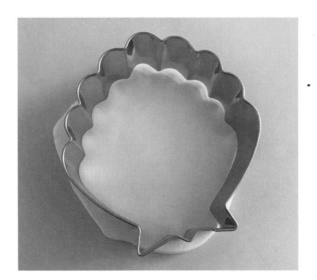

3. Place your shell cutter on the Fimo and press down hard. Remove any excess Fimo from around the side of the cutter. Use a spatula to pick up the shell so you don't stretch it out the shape.

4. Put the Fimo shape in the palm of your hand and curve it gently, without pulling it out of shape. Bend the scalloped edges up slightly by pushing them in towards the centre of the shell.

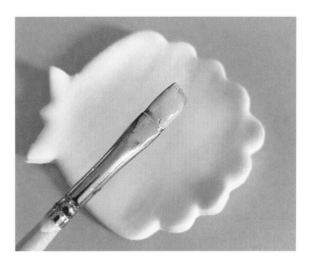

5. Once you are happy with your shell shapes, place them on an oven proof dish ready to set in the oven. Bake the shapes for 35 minutes in the pre heated oven. Take them out and put them on a drying tray to cool down and harden.

6. Once the shapes have cooled down, you will find they are very hard and ready to decorate. Mix acrylic paint with water to a watery consistency that you can pick up easily with the paint brush. Load your brush ready to splatter your design.

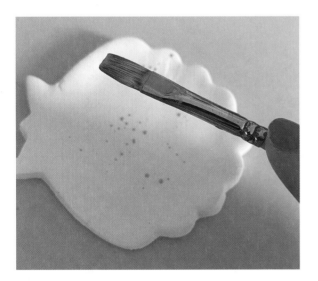

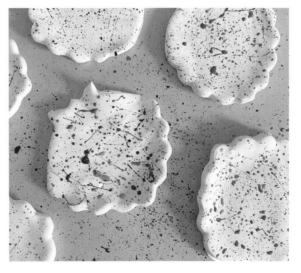

7. Begin lightly tapping the paint brush to create the splatter effect across your dish. If your paint is too watery you'll find it will just drip off the brush so practice using a spare piece of paper first. Have fun with this project.

8. There's no right or wrong way to splatter paint so enjoy creating your own effects on the shell shapes. Clean your brushes thoroughly if you use different colours to keep the colours clean. When finished, leave them to dry overnight and they're ready to use.

citrus linen tablecloth

Celebrate the joy of summer by making your own table linen with a citrus inspired design. Using paint, a potato and a simple stitch technique you can create this fun table cloth perfect for warm sunshine evenings in the garden with friends and nibbles. Style with brightly coloured glassware and fresh flowers.

Materials:

■ Linen tablecloth

■ Tulip Soft Matte Fabric Paint in orange

■ A potato

■ Mixing bowl

■ Flat paintbrush

■ Green embroidery thread

■ Embroidery needle

BECKI'S TIPS

■ You may find it easier to pop your fabric in an embroidery hoop to pull the fabric tight whilst embroidering the motifs. If you don't have one, just be careful not to pull the thread too tightly and pucker the material

■ Check whether your fabric paint needs to be fixed before washing

■ I'd advise hand washing or cold washing the table cloth

■ If you have limited time, make a table runner or napkins instead

67

1. Before you get started it is a good idea to iron your fabric to make the printing as easy as possible. Make sure you mix enough fabric paint for the whole project, so you don't have an issue with trying to recreate the colour half way through. Fill your mixing bowl with dye, so it is ready to work from.

2. Cut your potato in half to create a printing block. Use a flat paint brush to paint a thin even layer of fabric paint over the potato. If this is your first time printing, have a couple of practice goes on a piece of paper first to make sure you are confident with how much paint you need to create a even print.

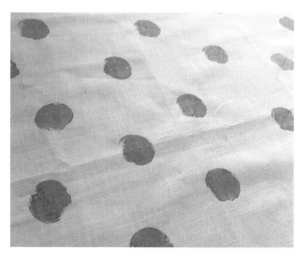

3. Use your potato to create orange prints. I find it easier to start at the side of the fabric and work across from top to bottom. Whilst you don't want your pattern to look too ordered, you do need to consider the spaces between your shapes.

4. If any of your prints are a bit light, print over them again with the potato. I personally like the imperfect nature of printing and like each of my prints to look a little different. Once you are happy with your printing, leave your fabric to dry.

5. Take a pencil and draw leaves on each of the printed orange circles. Make a mix of symmetrical and asymmetrical leaves for an authentic look. Make sure your leaves point in different directions.

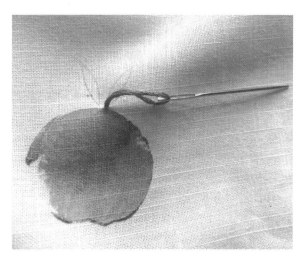

6. Thread an embroidery needle with green embroidery thread, tie a knot in one end and start stitching the leaves by starting at the bottom of each leaf shape.

7. Make one long stitch from the top to the bottom of the leaf. This is called a long stitch and is the only stitch you'll need for this project. Repeat this stitch to fill in the leaf shape working your long stitches close together to cover the whole shape.

8. Repeat on each motif remembering to knot the thread on each leaf as you go. Embroider each motif separately to prevent lots of embroidery thread showing at the back. Give the table cloth a good iron and it's ready to use.

chapter six: autumn

As we ease into the shorter days, I look once again to nature
for inspiration for my colour palettes and the projects I create.
The falling leaves create carpets of auburn, yellow and orange,
pumpkins and squash are in season and it is a wonderful
time to cook with seasonal produce. There is nothing more
quintessentially autumnal than a walk, kicking your feet through
the carpet of leaves, before coming home for soup and crusty
bread. The projects in this chapter reflect home, cosiness and the
warm colours of autumn. Try making your own candleholders,
printing with leaves, or painting a pumpkin.

wabi-sabi candlesticks

Enjoy using clay with these Wabi-sabi inspired candlestick holders. With a mix of heights and sizes you can create a lovely display of candles to create a pretty display on your mantelpiece, shelf or as a table centrepiece.

Materials:

- Air dry clay
- Candle
- Acrylic paint
- Paint brush
- Pot of water

BECKI'S TIPS
- You can use varnish to coat the holders. However, because they don't come into contact with food or water, it is fine to leave them unvarnished

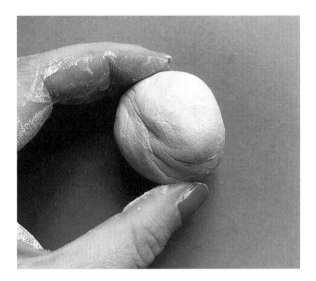

1. Begin by choosing your colour palette. I picked rich autumn inspired colours, with electric blue for contrast. Protect your work surface with a piece of paper before you start.

2. Air drying clay is easy to work with. Take a piece about the size of a golf ball and roll it into a ball with your hands. Use your fingers to gently smooth the clay as you do so.

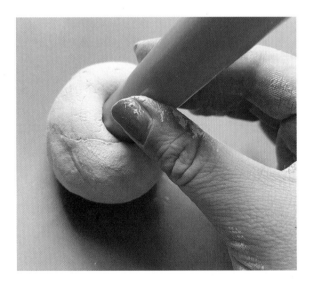

3. Press the clay down to create a flat bottom for your candlestick holder. Use a candle to make a hole deep enough for it to sit securely in the clay.

4. Smooth round the top of the candlestick holder by dipping your hands in water and then gently smoothing around the top edge with your finger tips.

5. You are now ready to dry your first candlestick holder. You can see that when you pushed the candle into the holder, it flatted and widened the shape so it looks less round ball-like. Don't worry if it looks uneven; that's the look you are going for.

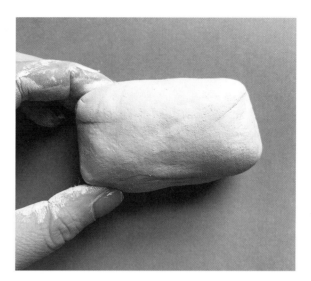

6. Take the next piece of clay and experiment with creating a different shape. Use the same technique to build the shape in your hand before creating a flattened bottom and then smoothing the surface with moistened fingertips.

7. Remember to use a candle to make an imprint in each candlestick holder before you leave them overnight to dry. The bigger the candlestick, the longer it will take to dry.

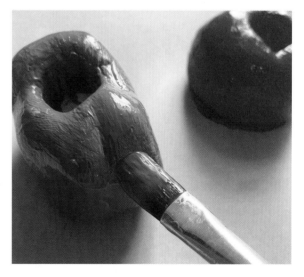

8. Paint the candlestick holders using a flat brush and acrylic paint. Paint both the outside and the inside so that when they are displayed without candles they look professional and well-finished.

graphic clay mobile

Create your own modern graphic wall hanging using clay and a painterly colour blocking technique to make abstract patterns. Use your own colour palette to create a unique piece to adorn your walls or make the perfect gift for a friend's house warming or a new baby.

Materials:

◻ Fimo Professional White Modelling Clay

◻ Cookie cutter

◻ Knife

◻ Metal straw

◻ Acrylic paint in your chosen colour palette

◻ Flat brush

◻ Black marker pen

◻ Dowel

◻ String

BECKI'S TIPS

◻ Use colours that complement the space you are making the piece for. Look around the room before you decide on your colour scheme.

◻ You could also use two dowels in an X-shaped cross to make a mobile style hanging

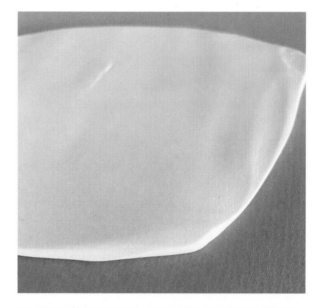

1. Pre-heat your oven to 110°C/230°F. Work on a clean dust-free surface as Fimo clay will absorb any dust or dirt it comes into contact with. Roll out two golf ball sized pieces of clay until it is about 1cm thick.

2. Using the cookie cutter upside down, press down on the clay and cut out six circle shapes. You can roll excess Fimo back into a ball to make more circles.

3. Cut some of your circular shapes in half using a sharp knife to ensure a smooth edge. You will then have a mixture of circles and half moon shapes.

4. Using the metal straw piece through the top of each shape to create a hole to hang it from. Do this before you bake your Fimo as you won't be able to once it's dry.

5. Place your shapes into a oven proof tray and put in the oven on the middle shelf for 30 minutes. Remove from the oven and leave on a drying rack to cool.

6. Fix washi tape tightly to your shapes in your desired pattern. This will ensure you create straight lines when you paint your blocks of colour

7. Apply paint over the clay on both sides. You will see both sides when the mobile moves around. You can also leave a few of the shapes blank to decorate with the a marker pens.

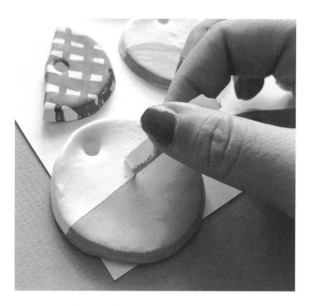

8. Remove the washi tape to reveal your clean paint lines. Do this in one clean movement to make sure you don't get excess paint anywhere and ruin all your hard work.

9. With a permanent marker pen, you can add simple patterns to the clay pieces. Simple dots and gingham designs work well to create modern patterns.

10. Attach string through the holes and tie your clay pieces to the dowel rod. Knot it securely and your mobile is ready to hang!

leaf printed napkins

Bring the outside in and celebrate autumn by inviting friends over for pumpkin soup at a table laid with your own printed napkins. If you enjoy sewing, you can make your own napkins from scratch or you can upcycle old linen napkins with this pretty seasonal design.

Materials:

- Dark linen fabric (27x40cm/11x16"per napkin)
- Needle and thread or sewing machine
- Pins
- White fabric paint
- Paint brush
- Mixing tray
- Paint roller
- Scrap paper
- Leaves of your choice

BECKI'S TIPS

- If you are using a dark linen, you will need to use a white or cream colour as darker colours won't show up enough detail

- If you are using shop bought or vintage napkins you already own, make sure the fabric is suitable for fabric paint. Linen and cotton works best.

This project can get messy so it is advisable to protect your work surface with newspaper before you start. I find it easier to make several napkins out of one piece of material rather than cutting it down to individual napkin sizes first. This piece of linen is 30cm/12" wide and 160cm/63" long. If you don't have the space to do this, it's fine to cut each napkin out first.

1. Spread a dollop of paint in your mixing tray using a paint brush. It is easier to start with a small amount of paint and add more so just cover the bottom of the tray with a small amount to start with.

2. Place your leaf down in the tray and use the brush to cover it in paint in an even layer. Make sure the paint is thin enough that you can still see some of the detail of the leaf. Don't worry if you get messy!

3. Place the leaf at the edge of the fabric to make your first print. Practice on excess material or paper beforehand if you like. However, as each print depends on the amount of paint and the pressure you apply, it's not always helpful.

4. Place a piece of paper over your leaf and roll over it, applying pressure. The paper helps ensure you don't spread any excess paint from the top of the leaf on to the fabric. Remove the paper and the leaf to reveal your first print.

5. Repeat this printing process across the fabric. Use plenty of fresh sheets of paper to make sure you don't accidentally spread paint onto your fabric. If you are feeling confident, you can print a few leaves onto the fabric at the same time.

6. Make sure you print some partial leaves on the edges of your fabric to make the pattern look even. This is much easier to achieve if you work on a larger piece of material than if you print on smaller napkin sized pieces.

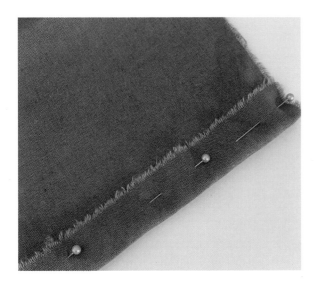

7. Once you have finished printing, cut your fabric to 40x40cm/16x16" wide. Create a small seam allowance and press it. Stitch a small hem around the napkin using a zig zag stitch on a sewing machine or a running stitch by hand.

8. Fold in the corners for a neat finish. Once your napkins are hemmed, iron them and they are ready to use. I make about eight napkins for a full set.

white painted pumpkins

Give your pumpkins a whimsical makeover this Halloween with simple minimalist botanical paintings. Pop these on a shelf with a vase of dried grasses, tea lights and an autumnal branch to create a cosy display that celebrates the slowing down of the seasons.

Materials:

◻ Pumpkins

◻ White spray paint

◻ Posca Paint Marker

BECKI'S TIPS

◻ You can also use acrylic paint for this project; just make sure you use a rounded brush to create the precise line work you will need

◻ If white minimalism isn't your thing, you can use a coloured spray paint as a base colour to add some warmth to your design

1. Give your chosen pumpkins a good wipe with a wet cloth and then dry them so you have a clean surface to work on. If you can't find pumpkins, squashes are also a great alternative for this project.

2. Apply a layer of spray paint to each pumpkin. Work outside if you can, as the fumes from the spray paint can be quite intense. It is also a good idea to cover any work surfaces with paper to protect them.

3. Once your pumpkins are evenly covered, leave them to dry. Spray paint dries fairly quickly and you'll be able to quite easily tell by touch whether or not they are ready to paint on.

4. To create the first minimalist pumpkin design, you are aiming to create very simple graphic lines. Start by painting stems for your flowers. Odd numbers work best so try painting three intertwining stems.

5. Paint petal shapes at the end of each stem, making sure each petal overlaps the one next to it. If you feel a bit nervous about painting directly onto your pumpkin, use a pencil to sketch out your flower first.

6. The next pumpkin design consists of overlapping petals which all meet at a middle point. Vary the size of each petal for a less uniform look to your motifs. Draw in the centre of the flower at the end.

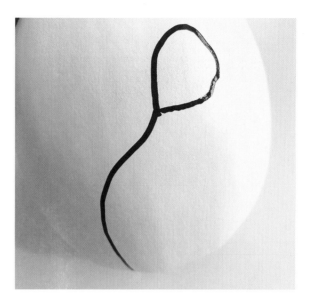

7. Repeat this motif to make cluster of flowers and then join them together with stems that meet at the bottom of the pumpkin. You can repeat these motifs to create a pattern all over the pumpkin or just stick to one motif in the middle.

8. The final design uses mixed motifs. Paint tall floral shapes; imagine your first one as a balloon shape and work from there to add more petals either side of your first petal shape.

9. Paint leaf shapes onto the stem. Try and let your pen wobble a little when drawing your leaves to give them a nice natural look - have a look at leaves in your garden for inspiration.

10. Add smaller floral shapes between the taller flowers by painting a soft wavy lined oval before adding the black centre with the paint pen. Your three pumpkin designs are done!

abstract flower vase

For me, autumn is all about the dried flowers and leaves that create such interesting shapes and silhouettes. This simple vase is inspired by the warm tones of autumn and the abstract shapes of branches empty of their leaves. Use it to display dried flowers and grasses.

Materials:

- Square vase

- Paint brush

- Acrylic paints in your chosen colours. I used green, mustard, brown, white and peach

- Sharpie marker

- Pencil

BECKI'S TIPS

- A square vase complements the curved lines of the design, however any size or shape of vase will work. Make sure the vase is glazed inside if you want to fill it with water

- You could also make this design using a Posca Paint Marker

- When you are bored with this design, just use white spray paint to spray over it and start again!

Decide on your colour palette, but focus on 3-4 colours. I chose autumnal colours and mixed them myself to make green, terracotta, brown, peach, white and mustard. Mix your colours to get the look you want.

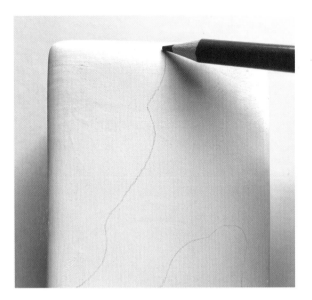

2. Using a pencil, draw abstract shapes on the vase. Use my design as inspiration or create your own. I find using something from nature helps me create a design - an oak leaf is a good place to start.

3. Begin colouring in your first shape using your chosen paint and a flat brush. Push it around the shape using pressure to create clean lines, particularly on any curved shapes.

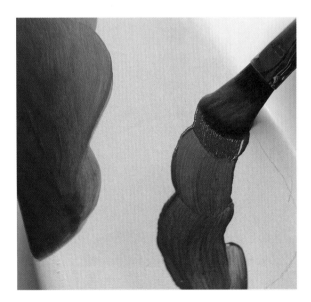

4. Paint bits of the first colour all around the vase to give the design a cohesive feel. Remember, with abstract shapes there's no wrong or right - just enjoy experimenting.

5. Bleed shapes off the side of the vase to give your design the look of an all over pattern, rather than motifs floating in the centre of a white space.

6. You can add another layer of colour onto your shapes to make the colour more opaque. Make sure your paint is dry first as acrylic paint will always look slightly darker once it has dried.

7. Using a permanent marker, begin to add groups of simple dots to your design. Don't fill all the white spaces. Let the white background create negative space in the design.

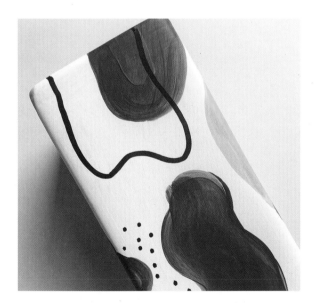

8. You can also draw outlines similar in shape to your coloured designs. If you find it easier, use a pencil to roughly plan your shapes first. Just be careful not to add too much detail and overcrowd your design.

9. When you are happy with your vase design, leave it to dry. Finally, apply a spray varnish if you want to make the vase waterproof. Then you are ready to fill it with water and your chosen flowers.

chapter seven: winter

'Tis the season for making! If you're organised you will have been crafting for Christmas since March, but if you are anything like me and have left it a little last minute the simple painterly crafts in this chapter will help celebrate the festive season. Try crafting your own wall hanging, complete with hand painted wreaths, paint your own gift wrap and create painted crackers for a naturally inspired Christmas table. It is the most magical time of the year and embracing the magic of the season is what helps me through the darker and shorter days. Find your festive joy and seasonal magic and hold onto it!

modern baubles

If you're a fan of the modern Scandi Christmas look, you'll love these monochrome baubles. With their gold finish and simple twine, they will transform your tree into a contemporary design statement. They also make great little handmade personalised gifts for the festive season.

Materials:

- Ceramic baubles
- Black Posca Paint Marker PC-5M
- Pebeo Gilding Wax in Empire Gold
- Flat paint brush
- Pencil

BECKI'S TIPS

- Use the twine provided with your baubles to help you hold them while you are painting them.

- For a Scandi look, change the jute for luxury white and black ribbons

- If you'd prefer to work with a colour base, spray paint the ceramics as it will dry a lot quicker and provide a smoother coverage for your painting than acrylic paint

- If you prefer more of a traditional and colourful decoration, there is another bauble decorating project in this seasonal chapter

95

1. Use the Posca Paint Marker to paint your initial onto the centre of the bauble. You could even paint full names onto the bauble if you are feeling confident. Do this personalisation step first and create your design around it.

2. Draw large spots around the bauble trying to keep them equidistant from each other to create a balanced polka dot pattern. Be careful as you work around the bauble; you'll need to allow time for the paint to dry or you will smudge it.

3. For a different effect, draw smaller dots using just the tip of the Paint Marker. These were created using the PC-5M Paint Marker. If you dab gently you will create a ditzier and smaller polka dot.

4. Triangles also make an effective design. When you are painting your patterns, the most important thing is to keep the spacing between the shapes even to ensure your design look clean.

5. Now it's time to get creative with the gliding wax. Wax is thick and heavily pigmented and creates a really opaque and vibrant look on your ceramic.

6. Use a pencil to make a rough mark where you want your gilding to finish. Begin painting from the underneath upwards with your gold gilding wax.

7. Use a flat brush to create a crisp line around the bottom of the bauble. Use pressure to drag the wax across the bauble, rather than applying too much and smearing it around.

8. The gold will need time to dry so hang your bauble up or pop it back in the box upside down so the bottom can dry. You will be able to tell by touch when they are dry and ready to hang.

classic baubles

If you love traditional Christmas decorations, these are the baubles for you. Create simple motifs in limited colour palettes on a set of tree decorations you'll want to treasure forever. If you are feeling generous, you could always make a set to give as a keepsake Christmas present.

Materials:

■ Ceramic baubles

■ Pencil

■ Watercolour paints

■ Round paint brush

BECKI'S TIPS

■ Place your baubles in an egg cup to make it easy to paint them

■ Add luxury velvet ribbons to hang the baubles to the tree

■ These motifs would look great in any colour so match them to your Christmas colour scheme

1. For the first design, you will need to draw four curved lines around your bauble with a 3cm/1" gap between them. Keep your guide pencil lines light; you don't want them to be visible through the paint.

2. Paint your first piece of foliage using a round brush. Be confident and draw the line in one sweeping stroke. Don't overload your brush with paint or you'll end up with a line that is thick at the top and thin at the bottom.

3. Draw the leaves with two strokes of the brush. Make a stroke downwards until you create a point and then move the brush back up. Press on the brush to distribute the paint into a leaf shape.

4. Repeat around the bauble to create a foliage frame on the front of the bauble. Be careful to make sure your painting is dry before you put your bauble down; you don't want to smudge your design.

5. The floral shape is made up of three oval shapes joined together at the base. Draw the shape out with a pencil first if you find it useful. You can then confidentially paint the colour over the top.

6. Paint two more foliage stems underneath the floral design, working outwards from the flower head in opposite directions to give a dynamic sense of movement to the design.

7. Add shorter lines around the motif to create the berry branches. Using a deeper colour, add dots along these branches to create depth. Using the tip of your brush, press down lightly on the bauble.

8. You can now add your berries to the foliage frame. I used the same colours as I chose for my main flower and then added more berries in a contrasting red to add more colour to my design.

9. The second design is created by repeating the foliage branch design in difference directions across the bauble. Just be careful as you work around the bauble that you let the motifs dry.

10. For the final design, begin in the middle of the bauble and draw large berries using a flat brush. Repeat the berry motif on the other side of the bauble, leaving enough space for your foliage designs.

11. Add two stems to the design. Then you are ready to add your bushy foliage shapes.

12. Add bushy foliage and simple leaves around your berries on both sides of your bauble. That's it!

foliage crackers

Inspired by my love of nature, delicate hand-painted Christmas crackers make the perfect show stopper for a festive table. Pair with soft linen ribbons, artisan plates, pretty glassware and an abundance of foliage for a pretty, contemporary Christmas table setting.

Materials:

■ 160gsm card

■ Green watercolour paint

■ Paint brush

■ Pot of water

■ Glue stick

■ Scissors or craft knife and cutting mat

■ String

■ Ribbon

BECKI'S TIPS

■ Add luxury ribbons to each end of the cracker to match your Christmas table theme

■ Cutting out the crackers is the most time-consuming part of this project. I like to put a Christmas film on and sit down to do my cutting in front of it. It's part of my Christmas ritual.

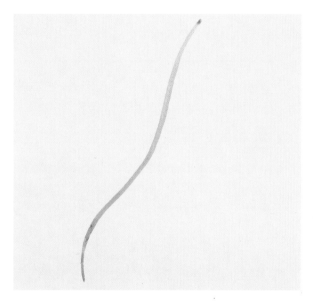

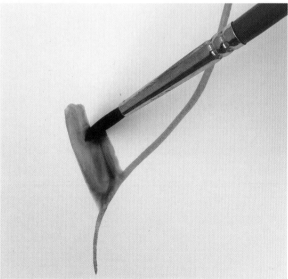

1. Begin by painting your design on the card. The foliage pattern is made up of one simple motif that you will repeat across the page. Start by painting a loose waved line that is around 7cm/3" long across the page.

2. To create the whimsical watercolour feel to the painting, you will need to dilute your paint with a lot of water. Use your brush to spread the paint into leaf shapes.

103

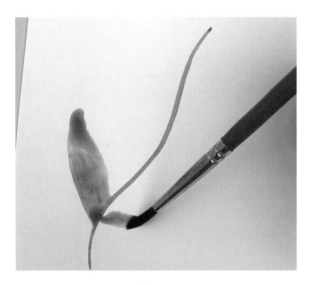

3. Simply repeat the leaf shapes up the stem. Drag your brush upwards first to a tip and then back down to the stem. Don't worry about painting perfectly symmetrical leaves; a loose style with differences in your leaf sizes and shapes is fine.

4. Repeat your leaf designs across the card, making sure you bleed the design off the edges to create an all-over pattern. Don't worry too much about creating equidistance between the leaves. You can fill any awkward spaces with the next layer of paint.

5. Once you have painted the first layer of leaves, you can then add the darker leaves. These leaves are created by diluting the paint colour less to achieve a more pigmented look.

6. Add darker leaves on each of the motifs. You'll see having different depths of colour creates a more delicate pattern which suits watercolour paints.

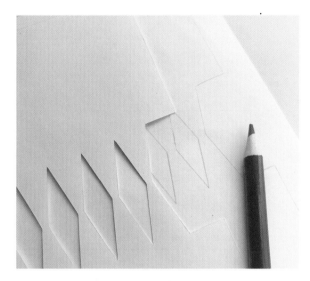

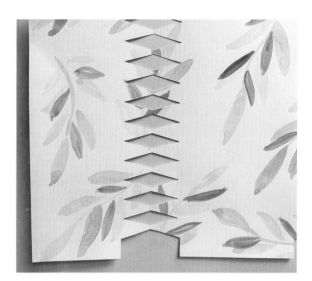

7. Make sure your sheets of patterns are dry and then put them paint side down on a table. Cut out the template on Page 114 and trace it onto the plain side of your card.

8. Cut out your crackers using a craft knife on a cutting mat. If you don't have a cutting mat and knife you can also use scissors to cut out your template.

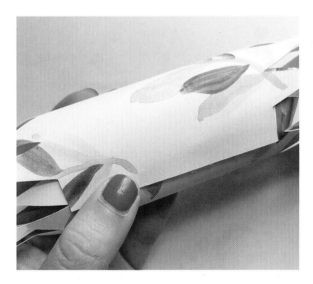

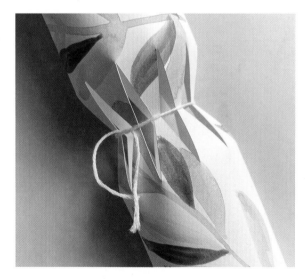

9. Roll the card to create your cracker. The size of the cracker is dependent on how tightly you roll the card. Glue along the flaps before pressing down to secure in place. If you wish to fill the crackers, add in your treat now.

10. Use a thin string to secure each end of the cracker, pulling it tight and tying in a knot. This will secure your cracker. Add your decorative ribbon over the top in a contrasting colour.

seasonal wall hanging

Paint and make your own festive wall hanging, perfect for Christmas celebrations. If you use words that have all year round meaning, you can keep them up long after the festivities are over.

Materials:

- ◼ Linen (the banners are 40x25cm/16x10") and matching thread
- ◼ Wooden dowel
- ◼ Needle and thread or sewing machine
- ◼ White Posca Paint Marker
- ◼ Round plate

BECKI'S TIPS

◼ Iron your fabric before you start. This will make it easier for you to paint on. You wouldn't start painting on a crumpled piece of paper so the same applies with fabric

◼ You can also use acrylic or fabric paints for this project; just make sure you use a round tipped paint brush for precision

◼ Add foliage around the top of the banners for extra texture to the piece

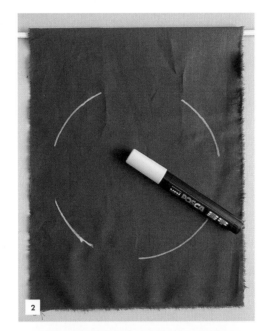

1. Cut the fabric to your rectangle shape. Mine are 40x25cm/16x10" in width but they can be any size, especially if you already have some fabric you'd like to use up. Fold the fabric over the dowel to check you're happy with the banner size.

2. Using the plate as a template, paint four curved lines using the Paint Marker. You want there to be a gap between the lines rather than one complete circle as you'll be adding motifs.

3. Each of the four curved lines are stems. Paint leaf shapes along them. These are simply made up of two curved lines meeting together at a point. Then add curved lines at the top of the stem for the berry branches.

4. Begin to add your circular berry shapes. Leave a little unpainted area to act as a shadow. Add an abundance of berries around your stems.

5. Repeat on all four stems, mixing the placement of the berries rather than trying to make them even. This will give the banner a more whimsical feel.

6. Add leaf shapes in the gaps between each stem of foliage. Add dots around the leaves by pushing the Paint Marker down on the fabric. Repeat on each of the four spaces between the foliage stems.

7. To add a word in the middle of your banner use a ruler to find the centre of your circle. This is where the centre of your word will sit. Joy is a perfect word as it has a nice symmetry.

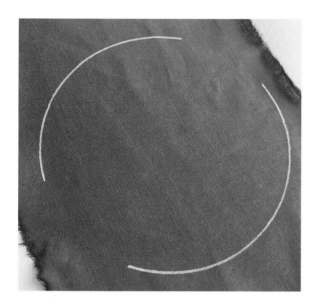

8. The next design involves drawing just two circular lines around your plate. Once again these will act as stem to add leaf shaped designs to.

9. Paint your leaf shapes and colour them in. You can paint smaller leaves in between the bigger leaves to create a dynamic design.

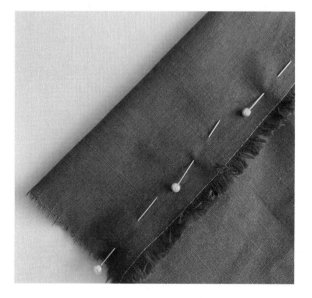

10. Add dots in between your leaf shapes with the Paint Marker, grouping them together in clusters to create berries. Odd numbers work well visually so paint groups of three or five berries.

11. Once you are happy with your designs, turn over a hem in your fabric and sew it up. Pop your dowel through the top and hang your wall hanging with ribbon ready to celebrate the festive season.

winter wrapping paper

We all know gifts aren't important; it is the magic of sharing and celebrating with friends and family that makes the festive season so special. Little handmade gestures, like making your own wrapping paper, are the little things that bring the greatest joy and happiness.

Materials:

■ Kraft Brown Paper

■ Posca Paint Marker PC-5M in white

■ Posca Paint Marker PC-5M in navy

■ Envelope

BECKI'S TIPS

■ This project is one of the more time consuming projects in the book. Don't overwhelm yourself by trying to paint a whole 2m roll. Just focus on making small book sized bits.

■ You can save time by wrapping your present with brown paper first and then paint your design over the wrapped gift

■ Mix up the sizes of your motifs to create a more interesting pattern. You can use a pencil to mark out your design first

■ You can use a roll of white paper and coloured Paint Markers if you'd prefer it to brown paper

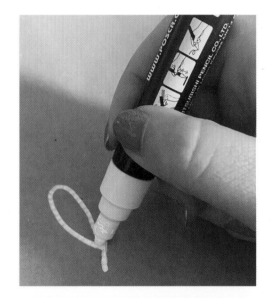

1. Creating wrapping paper designs can be as simple as repeating one motif across the paper. The key in making your design work is ensuring your motif is consistent. It is just a case of practicing the shape and feeling confident in painting it multiple times.

2. For this design, paint a curved line approx 7cm/3" long and then draw teardrop shapes along the length. Try and keep the size of the opposite leaves the same and pointing in the same direction.

111

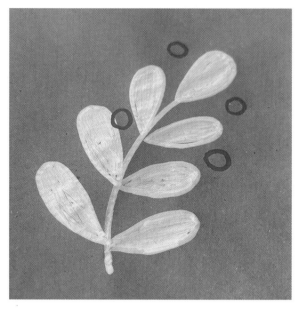

3. Colour in the leaf shape. Posca Paint Markers are opaque so you can outline your designs first and then fill them in without seeing any unsightly lines.

4. Using the blue Posca Paint Marker draw circles for berries. A mixture of berries sitting on the foliage and free floating around it looks best.

5. Colour in the berry shapes leaving a small circle unpainted. This gives the berries a 3D effect and helps the design look less flat.

6. Repeat the motif across the paper, trying to keep them equidistant from each other. Once dry the wrap is ready for your gifts!

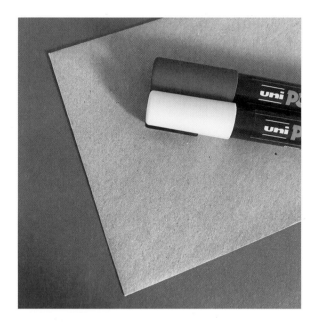

7. For personalised gift wrap, you can also add the same motifs to your cards. If you use brown Kraft paper try and find brown Kraft envelopes to match.

8. Start by writing the recipients' name in the middle of your card using the Posca Paint Marker to create a middle point to work around.

9. Draw the foliage design curving over the top and bottom of the name. Plan out the length of the foliage to fit around the length of the name.

10. Add berry shapes and you have the perfect matching envelope for our gift. It's a little handmade gesture that goes a long way!

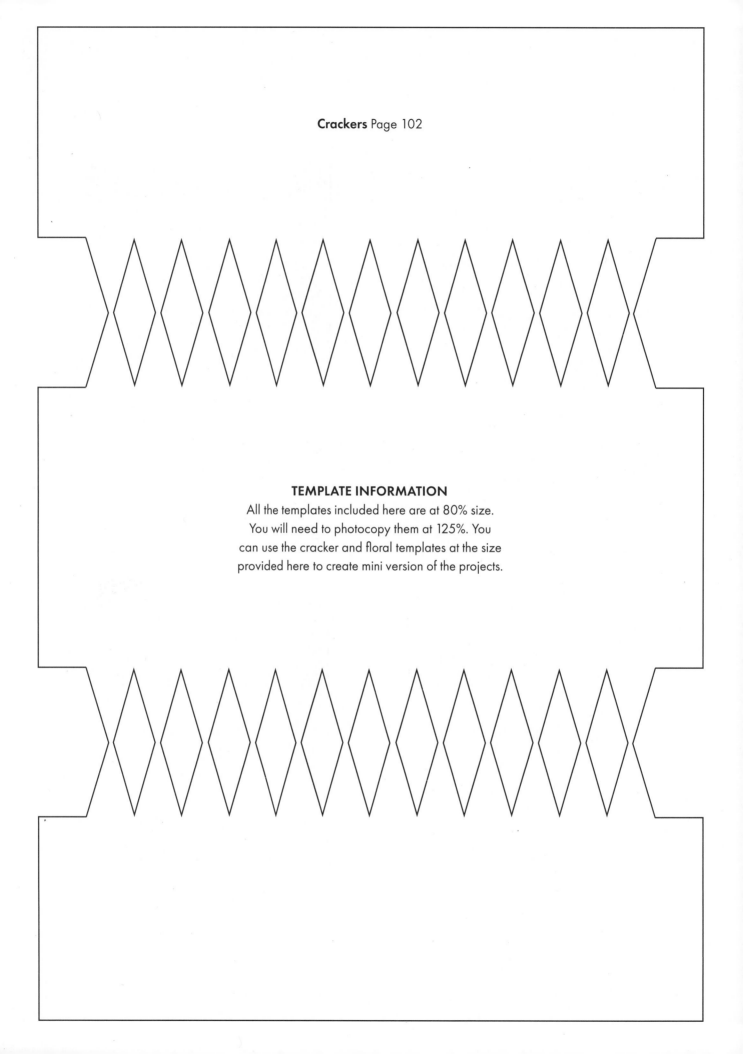

TEMPLATE INFORMATION
All the templates included here are at 80% size.
You will need to photocopy them at 125%. You
can use the cracker and floral templates at the size
provided here to create mini version of the projects.

**Collage
Shapes**
Page 32

**Cake Topper
Leaves** Page 23

frequently asked questions

I didn't study art. Will I still be able to paint?
Lots of people come along to my workshops or message me on Instagram saying they want to learn to paint but didn't study art so don't think they will be able to. Guess what? I only studied art up until GCSE and then gave it up to specialise in textiles and graphics. Although these are creative subjects I have never learnt how to paint in an academic environment. If you feel you want to paint that's a great place to start - just grab a paint brush and start working through some of the exercises at the start of the book and you'll soon feel confident handling a paint brush and using paints.

I'm finding it hard to find colour palettes I like. Where's the best place to start?
To begin with have a look around your home or your wardrobe and see what colours you are drawn to. You can also shut your eyes and try and imagine something you enjoyed doing. Painting and creating from joy is a great way to find a colour palette you love. Look at nature too; it's a great place to find colours that work together effortlessly. Use sites like Pinterest and save pictures you like on Instagram. You'll soon see colours you keep coming back to and get a feel for what your favourite colours are.

I'm left handed, will I find painting harder?
Not at all! All of the same principles apply throughout the book. I would just advise when working in a sketchbook or on paper that you work across from the right hand side of the paper to the left hand side so you don't end up with paint all over your hands. Having said that, I'm right handed and I still always end up with paint all over me.

I'm nervous about working on some of the surfaces that aren't flat. Any top tips?
This is quite a common question. It is different working across curved surfaces or even surfaces that feel different to touch than a flat piece of paper. Don't be put off. My advice is to use a pencil to sketch your design out lightly on to the surface you are going to paint on so you aren't working blindly.

What can I do after this book to keep up my painting hobby?
I really hope you want to continue your painting journey after reading and crafting your way through this book. I recommend taking your paints and a sketchbook and doing some real life observations. Sit in a park, a local cafe, your garden or even in your own living room and look for interesting shapes, colour combinations and objects to paint. Explore breaking down objects into simple shapes to paint and finding your own way of creating painterly motifs and designs. If you want to learn more from me I run botanical painting workshops which focus on painting with watercolours to create illustrative floral, fauna and nature inspired work.

I don't want to spend a lot of money to start with, what do you recommd buying?
You can buy most paints by the pan or tube meaning you can just purchase the colours you want to work with. Brushes can also be bought singularly and card and paper is sold by the sheet in art shops.

If you have any other questions then message me on Instagram @becki_clark_ and I will reply to you there.

stockists and resources

You don't need a lot of specialist materials, however it's important to invest in good quality paints and brushes as they will last much longer than cheaper alternatives. You can get started with a set of paints and a couple of different brushes.

Watercolour Paints
- Windsor & Newton 12 Half Pans You'll be able to complete any of the watercolour projects in this book using this set.

Acrylic Paints
- Daler Rowney Graduate Acrylic Paint 9 Pack is a perfect first set.

Paint Markers
- Any of the Posca Paint Markers are good. You can buy colours individually or as larger sets.

Brushes
- Daler Rowney Gold Taklon Long Handled Brushes 10 Pack
- Daler Rowney Long Handle Bristle Filbert Graduate Brush Size 8 White
- Daler Rowney Round Brush Size 1

Paper & Card
Each project specifies the paper or card you need, but some good general pads to have in your painter's box are:
- Hobbycraft Watercolour Paper Pad A4 (perfect for practising with watercolours)
- Hobbycraft A4 Jumbo Drawing Pad 150 Sheets (great for Posca Pens and acrylics as the paper is smooth rather than grainy)
- 300gsm smooth card

My favourite shops to buy from:
Hobbycraft is a great place to start for painting supplies; they stock all the materials listed as well as single tubes of acrylic, watercolour and gouache paint, perfect for when you have a specific colour palette in mind. They also stock all the other craft materials you need for each project.

About the author

Becki Clark is a multidisciplinary creative designer based in the New Forest with over eight years experience in the creative industry. Inspired by flora and fauna and nature's seasonality, Becki's signature painterly style lends itself to a vast range of projects, from botanical painting and brush lettering, to surface pattern design. Her distinctive style has led to collaborations with Hobbycraft, Seasalt Cornwall and BBC's Countryfile. Becki's work also often features in print editorial, including magazines like Mollie Makes, Homes & Antiques and In The Moment.

Becki regularly hosts sell-out workshops teaching botanical painting, brush lettering and crafting for both individuals and for brands such as Daylesford Farm, Homesense, Soho House and Pukka Herbs.

In her first book, 'Modern Brush Lettering', Becki created a beginner's guide to the art of brush lettering, plus 20 seasonal projects to showcase her signature lettering style.

In recent years Becki has also extended her portfolio to include print and pattern design, and licensed print design for homewares, stationery, textiles and packaging.

At the weekend, you'll find Becki out walking in the New Forest looking for inspiration, reading, cooking or making flower displays around her beautiful home.

Acknowledgements
I'd like to thank Katherine Raderecht, Jane Toft and Jesse Wild for their support and creative input into this book. It was a delight to work with such a great team once again. I am especially grateful to Katherine for her continued encouragement. Thank you also to Hobbycraft for supplying all of the materials for the book, as well as all the wonderful crafty friends on Instagram and in real life who have inspired me, cheered me on and encouraged me. A massive thank you to Laura who I love working with and who makes me laugh. www.beckiclark.com @becki_clark_